VAN HALEN

TRIVIA BOOK

Uncover The Epic History With Facts &
Trivia Questions!

By Dale Raynes

Bridge Press
dp@purplelink.org

Please consider writing a review!
Just visit: purplelink.org/review

Copyright 2021. Dale Raynes. All Rights Reserved.
No part of this book may be reproduced or transmitted in any
form or by any means, electronic or mechanical, including
photocopying, recording or by any other form without
written permission from the publisher.

ISBN: 978-1-955149-04-4

TABLE OF CONTENTS

INTRODUCTION

Van Halen is an American band known for bringing hard rock back into the spotlight in the late 1970s. As the disco craze took over the face of music during this time, Van Halen went a different direction and thrust a regenerated form of heavy metal rock to the forefront of popular culture. Previous bands had produced talented lead guitarists and begun to remake the classic rock of the '60s, but Van Halen transformed the genre by adding new wave and punk rock influences to traditional tones.

The end result cleared the path for a new generation of metal and hard rock. In particular, the graceful and technically unparalleled guitar playing of Eddie Van Halen had a seismic impact on the world of rock, causing it to transcend beyond its known sub-genres at that time. The strutting hair rock of Mötley Crüe, the shredding of Joe Satriani, and the sonic attack of the New Wave of British Heavy Metal would all have been impossible without Van Halen.

But more than anything else, Van Halen was just a fun band. Songs like "Jump" and "Runnin' with the Devil" could make even the most awkward people tap along to their irresistible beat. Van Halen also stood out as a tremendously dynamic and wild live act. Their shows had to be seen to be believed. All in all, Van Halen's rise to fame was nothing short of legendary.

The band's celebrated music was largely popular throughout the mid-1970s and '80s. Upon officially disbanding in 2020, the band had been playing together for upwards of 40 years. Their projected aesthetic of disregarding the rules and staying true to themselves, regardless of critics, has appealed to Americans far and wide.

To remind us of Van Halen's beginning, middle, end, and every tidbit in between, *Van Halen History & Trivia* is here to explore the legacy of this long-lived rock group.

This trivia book reviews the origins and influences that created Van Halen up through the current state of the band today. While the pinnacle of the band's career is behind us, the historical facts presented are up to date as of early 2021, and should remain mostly unchanged. Van Halen's most recent original content was released in 2012, though the statistics and figures mentioned may have fluctuated with remastering and special releases. The group was officially disbanded in November of 2020, one month after the death of lead guitarist Eddie Van Halen.

Use this book to evaluate your knowledge of the acclaimed band, with rounds of trivia covering various topics from throughout Van Halen's history. Whether you consider yourself a diehard fan or are just vaguely familiar with the band, this book will help you assess how much you really know about Van Halen and enlighten you with interesting facts.

Let's "Jump" in and see how much you really know about Van Halen!

CHAPTER 1:

BACK TO THE BEGINNING

TRIVIA TIME!

1. In which city were the Van Halen brothers, Alex and Eddie, born?

    a. London, England
    b. Stockholm, Sweden
    c. Amsterdam, The Netherlands
    d. Brussels, Belgium

2. Which of the following was the first name used by Van Halen?

    a. The Snapped Brushes
    b. The Broken Combs
    c. The Shattered Glass
    d. The Splintered Hairbrushes

3. In which year did the band name become known as Van Halen?

    a. 1972

b. 1970

c. 1974

d. 1980

4. True or False: When the band was named Genesis, they were forced to change it after it was discovered that the name was already in use by a popular British group.

5. Which instruments did Alex and Eddie play in the 1960s?
    a. Alex on drums, Eddie on guitar
    b. Lead singer Eddie, Alex on guitar
    c. Eddie on drums, Alex on guitar
    d. Lead singer Alex, Eddie on drums

6. True or False: The Van Halen brothers began playing different instruments but then switched with each other, which became the familiar lineup today.

7. Which of these was also a previous name of the band?
    a. Mammoth
    b. Elephant
    c. Hippopotamus
    d. Rhinoceros

8. Lead vocalist David Lee Roth was introduced to the band when he…
    a. Noticed the Van Halen brothers playing in a club
    b. Lent the brothers a sound system
    c. Was told by a friend to audition for the band
    d. Was a young child

9. True or False: When Van Halen performed live, there were often noise complaints and traffic jams.

10. True or False: After releasing their first single, Van Halen hit #1 on the *Billboard* pop music charts.

11. Eddie Van Halen's guitar technique was referred to as:
    a. "Finger-tapping"
    b. "Hand-beating"
    c. "Finger-jabbing"
    d. "Hand-pattering"

12. True or False: Van Halen used to open for the Rolling Stones.

13. What was the name of the band's first top 20 single?
    a. "Eruption"
    b. "Runnin' with the Devil"
    c. "Jump"
    d. "Dance the Night Away"

14. In which year did the band release its first album?
    a. 1974
    b. 1978
    c. 1980
    d. 1972

15. True or False: Van Halen's first tour left the band over $1 million in debt.

16. Who produced the band's demo tape?

a. Gene Simmons of KISS
b. David Lee Roth
c. Ozzy Osborne of Black Sabbath
d. Ronnie Van Zant of Lynyrd Skynyrd

17. The manager who signed them was also involved with which band?
    a. The Sex Pistols
    b. The Beatles
    c. AC/DC
    d. Led Zeppelin

18. True or False: Gene Simmons suggested changing the band name to Daddy Longlegs.

19. Van Halen's album *Women and Children First* reached which level of status?
    a. Gold
    b. Multi-Platinum
    c. Silver
    d. Diamond

20. Which record company first signed Van Halen?
    a. Warner Bros. Records
    b. Sony Music Entertainment
    c. Universal Music Group
    d. Warner Music Group

ANSWERS:

1. C

2. B

3. C

4. True

5. C

6. True

7. A

8. B

9. True

10. False

11. A

12. False

13. D

14. B

15. True — Unfortunately for Van Halen

16. A

17. A

18. True

19. B

20. A

DID YOU KNOW?

- The Van Halen brothers first began performing together when Eddie was in just the fourth grade. He and Alex, along with three other boys, played at their school during lunch period at Hamilton Elementary.

- The Van Halen Brothers, Alex and Eddie, were the only two continuous band members from beginning to end. Other members came and went, most notably David Lee Roth, who left to pursue a solo career.

- According to former band member David Lee Roth, it was his idea to change the band name to Van Halen. After rotating through several names, the band decided to be called Mammoth. However, they received a cease-and-desist order from a San Fernando music group with the same name. Both Eddie and Alex wanted to change the name to "Rat Salad" as a nod to Black Sabbath, who they frequently opened for. Roth insisted that the name Van Halen left a more lasting impression, and so it was used.

- The band was discovered by a major record label on February 2nd, 1977, when producer Ted Templeman and record executive Mo Ostin of Warner Brothers watched them play in Hollywood's Starwood Club. Ostin offered them a record deal the very next day.

- Brothers Alex and Eddie Van Halen both began playing instruments at an incredibly young age. As a child, Eddie Van Halen could not read music, but won an annual piano recital contest several years in a row.

- Alex and Eddie Van Halen were first introduced to music by their father, Jan Van Halen, who was a jazz musician. Born in the Netherlands in 1920, Jan Van Halen became skilled on both the saxophone and clarinet before he was 18.

- While both Alex and Eddie were born in the Netherlands, the Van Halen family decided to move from Amsterdam to the United States, where they settled in Pasadena, California.

- Gene Simmons has stated how, during this period of the 1970s, people in the music scene were constantly scouting for and finding new bands. Despite this sea of talented new musicians and groups, Simmons claims Van Halen captured his attention like none other.

- Jan Van Halen, Eddie and Alex's father, enlisted in the Dutch Air Force in 1939 before the turmoil of WWII. His musical talent was put to use in the Air Force Band.

- Alex and Eddie were encouraged by their parents to become classical musicians, but both teenage boys were entranced with rock music.

- Van Halen recorded their first album with Gene Simmons in New York's Electric Ladyland Studios. The studio had been built by famous guitarist Jimi Hendrix.

- Jan Van Halen was captured by German troops when Germany invaded the Netherlands in only five days in 1940. Jan's musical talent allowed him to play propaganda music to entertain German troops instead of fighting in combat for Germany. The marching tunes he learned during this time left his young sons in awe of his musical talent, and inspired both boys to continue learning to play different instruments.

- After he discovered the band, Gene Simmons desperately wanted Bill Aucoin, the manager of his band KISS, to manage Van Halen. Unfortunately, KISS was about to begin a tour, and the other members could not understand why Simmons was so invested in the band. Simmons was forced to let Van Halen out of their contract. Shortly after, Van Halen was signed by Warner Bros.

- The band is a classic example of the "American Dream." The Van Halen family moved to the United States from the Netherlands with just $50, a piano, and no knowledge of the English language. Today, the brothers are world-renowned rock musicians.

CHAPTER 2:

A BAND IS BORN

TRIVIA TIME!

1. The band played together as Mammoth during which years?
   a. 1970-1971
   b. 1969-1970
   c. 1971-1973
   d. 1972-1974

2. The very first official lineup using the name Van Halen included...
   a. Alex, Eddie, David, Mark
   b. Alex, Eddie, David, Michael
   c. Alex, Eddie, Jan, Mark
   d. Alex, Eddie, Gene, Jan

3. Van Halen's first official performance as a headlining act was in which city?
   a. San Francisco, California

b. Las Vegas, Nevada

c. Santa Fe, New Mexico

d. Fresno, California

4. True or False: Gene Simmons of the band KISS was briefly a member of Van Halen between 1974 and 1975.

5. Van Halen's first tour was as the opening act for which popular rock band?
   a. Black Sabbath
   b. AC/DC
   c. KISS
   d. Journey

6. True or False: After touring with AC/DC in 1978, Van Halen was able to begin its own tour as the headline act.

7. Van Halen's very first album was titled which of the following?
   a. 1984
   b. Women and Children First
   c. Van Halen
   d. 5150

8. Van Halen's first top 40 single was titled...
   a. "You Really Got Me"
   b. "Ice Cream Man"
   c. "Somebody Get Me a Doctor"
   d. "On Fire"

9. The band's first world tour occurred in which year?

a. 1976
b. 1978
c. 1980
d. 1979

10. Before commercial success, Van Halen often played in which cities?
    a. Los Angeles, Las Vegas
    b. Pasadena, San Bernardino
    c. New York City, Philadelphia
    d. San Francisco, Sacramento

11. True or False: Gene Simmons was invited to watch Van Halen at the Sunset Strip club known as Gazzarri's.

12. Before joining Van Halen, Michael Anthony played for which lesser-known band?
    a. Lizard
    b. Snake
    c. Reptile
    d. Worm

13. In their early live performances, the band was often met with...
    a. Noise complaints
    b. Crowds of up to 2,000 people
    c. Traffic jams
    d. All of the above

14. Which other rock band had been "discovered" at Gazzarri's club?

a. The Doors
b. The Byrds
c. The Beach Boys
d. The Beatles

ANSWERS:

1. D
2. B
3. D
4. False
5. D
6. False
7. C
8. A
9. B
10. C
11. True
12. B
13. D
14. A

DID YOU KNOW?

- When Alex and Eddie Van Halen first began playing in their band, The Broken Combs, the band had five members total. They played alongside their classmates and childhood friends Brian Hill, Kevan Hill and Don Farris. Eddie was just 9 and Alex was all of 11 years old.

- Up until 2019, Van Halen's first performance on their world tour with Black Sabbath was considered "lost." Clips of the show had been made available over the years, but the recording of the full performance was recently posted to YouTube. The performance had been captured on an 8mm film camera with a reel that could only shoot up to three minutes, so there are gaps in the recording as the reel is changed.

- Before joining Van Halen, David Lee Roth was a member of the rock group Red Ball Jets. Mammoth (at the time consisting of Alex, Eddie, and Mark Stone) would rent the Red Ball Jets' sound system occasionally, which led to Roth's auditioning for the band and becoming the lead singer.

- The early music group The Broken Combs wrote several original songs despite their young age. Some included "Rumpus" and "Boogie Booger." They performed in the lunchroom at their elementary school.

- Alex and Eddie Van Halen met both David Lee Roth and Michael Anthony during their time at Pasadena City College.

- Record companies were originally reluctant to sign Van Halen for record deals. At the time, the disco genre was outshining hard rock.

- Before Van Halen's big break, the band built up a cult following in the local areas they played in. They were heavily invested in self-promotion, and the band would often hand out flyers at high schools.

- When Van Halen was given a permanent gig in 1974 at the Sunset Strip club Gazzari's, the band had two managers, Mark Algorri and Mario Miranda. The owner of Gazzari's complained that the band was too chaotic and loud, so Van Halen's managers assumed the role of booking, and scheduled the band to play up through 1976.

- After all the success the band experienced after performing at numerous popular local clubs, it was clear they needed a demo tape if they wanted to continue climbing the ladder to fame. Their first demo tape was recorded at David Lee Roth's home.

- Michael Anthony was originally hesitant to join the band as its bassist. At the time, he was a member of the music group Snake, which was more successful. Despite his reluctance, Anthony was encouraged by one of his Snake bandmates to seize the opportunity.

- After being rejected by the band KISS's management, Gene Simmons put Doug Messenger, the lead guitarist for musician Van Morrison, in contact with Van Halen. Messenger then contacted producer Ted Templeman of Warner Bros. Records. The record company was looking for a "guitar hero" act, and Van Halen fit the bill perfectly.

- Alex and Eddie Van Halen met one of their fellow members of The Broken Combs, Kevan Hill, in their morning music class in elementary school. Eddie played the violin while Kevan was extremely skilled on the cello. He and his brother Brian became fast friends with both Van Halen brothers.

- When Van Halen was known as Mammoth, bassist Michael Anthony's former band Snake would open for them. The two bands often played similar gigs at the same clubs and local venues.

- When producer Ted Templeman went to see Van Halen perform for the first time, it was the band's first gig at the Starwood Club in Hollywood. The next day he brought back record executive Mo Austin to see them too. The audience was small and consisted of only about 11 people. Despite the poor turnout, both Templeman and Ostin were blown away by Van Halen's performance, and soon after offered them a contract to record at Warner Bros. Records.

- David Lee Roth felt inspired by the music group Santana to name the band Van Halen. Roth wanted to have a memorable band name for marketing advantages.

- The band's first supporting tour featured the bands Journey and Montrose. This tour was part of the first record deal offered to Van Halen by Warner Bros.

- Representatives from Warner Bros. wrote a letter of intent to Van Halen on a napkin very soon after the show Mo Austin had seen. This preceded their first official meeting at a local diner, approximately one week after watching the band perform at the Starwood.

- Originally, Van Halen had considered hiring David Lee Roth as the lead singer despite failing his initial audition. However, Eddie hired him later when he decided he did not want to sing anymore.

- The very first record deal Van Halen was offered by Warner Bros. left the band with substantial debt. The record company only paid them $0.70 per album. However, they improved their contract after two years.

CHAPTER 3:

WHO'S WHO AND WHAT'S WHAT

TRIVIA TIME!

1. David Lee Roth was Van Halen's...
   a. Lead guitarist
   b. Bassist
   c. Pianist
   d. Lead vocalist

2. True or False: In 2006, Eddie Van Halen's son Wolfgang became a member and replaced bassist Michael Anthony.

3. Michael Anthony played which instrument?
   a. Drums
   b. Piano
   c. Guitar
   d. Bass

4. David Lee Roth briefly reunited with the band in which year?
   a. 1990
   b. 1986

c. 1993

d. 1996

5. From 2007 until Eddie's death in 2020, the most recent members of the band included…
   a. Alex, Eddie, David, Jan
   b. Alex, Eddie, Mark, Michael
   c. Alex, Eddie, Michael, Sammy
   d. Alex, Eddie, David, Wolfgang

6. David Lee Roth left the band in 1985 for which reason?
   a. He was kicked out
   b. He wanted to pursue a solo career
   c. He went to jail
   d. He became injured and could no longer perform

7. Who replaced lead singer David Lee Roth?
   a. Mitch Malloy
   b. Sammy Hagar
   c. Patty Smythe
   d. Gene Simmons

8. Lead singer Gary Cherone was a member of which other band?
   a. Extreme
   b. Ultimate
   c. Maximum
   d. Excessive

9. True or False: Bassist Mark Stone was replaced by Michael Anthony because Stone was hesitant about having a career in music.

10. David Lee Roth reunited briefly with the band during which award show?

    a. The Grammys
    b. The Oscars
    c. The MTV Music Awards
    d. The Emmys

11. Michael Anthony grew up in which city by the Van Halen brothers' hometown?

    a. San Francisco
    b. San Bernardino
    c. Arcadia
    d. Pasadena

12. In which year did Gary Cherone join Van Halen as the lead vocalist?

    a. 1994
    b. 1996
    c. 1998
    d. 1992

13. Another factor in David Lee Roth's departure from Van Halen was...

    a. His drug use
    b. His disagreements with the studio

c. Wanting to join a different band

d. His disagreements with Eddie

14. Sammy Hagar was a frontman for which band before Van Halen?

   a. KISS

   b. Montrose

   c. The Doors

   d. Led Zeppelin

15. People who watched the band perform live were mostly entranced by…

   a. Alex's drumming

   b. Michael's hot sauce

   c. Eddie's guitar skills

   d. The special effects

16. True or False: Van Halen took an unannounced hiatus between 1999 and 2003.

ANSWERS:

1. D
2. True
3. D
4. D
5. D
6. B
7. B
8. A
9. True
10. C
11. C
12. B
13. D
14. B
15. C
16. True

DID YOU KNOW?

- After David Lee Roth left Van Halen in 1985, the band struggled to replace him as lead vocalist. For a brief period of time, they considered other singers including Patty Smythe and Eric Martin. Eventually Eddie met solo artist Sammy Hagar, whom he had long appreciated, at a car mechanic's garage and offered him the job. He replaced Roth from 1985 up until 1996, when it's debated whether Hagar quit or was fired from the band.

- After Sammy Hagar departed the band, fans were thrilled when David Lee Roth decided to briefly reunite with Van Halen, and produced several new songs on the band's 1996 album *Best of – Volume I.*

- Bassist Michael Anthony's legal last name is "Sobolewski."

- Part of the motivation for Roth's leaving the band was receiving a $20 million film deal by CBS Pictures for a script he wrote titled *Crazy from the Heat.* He wanted to pursue his solo career and develop himself without being tied to the band. However, Roth wanted Van Halen to record some of the soundtrack for the movie. Eventually, the script was cancelled and the deal fell through.

- On September 4th, 1996, the band reunited with the four original members – Alex, Eddie, Michael, and David – to play during the MTV Music Awards. It was the first time the quartet had played together in 11 years.

- In his former band Snake, bassist Michael Anthony had also been lead vocalist.

- Eddie Van Halen was introduced to future band member Sammy Hagar when Van Halen opened for Montrose in Anaheim in 1978.

- After an unsuccessful reunion with David Lee Roth in 1996, the next lead vocalist for the band was Gary Cherone. With Cherone, Van Halen released the album *Van Halen III*. It is thought that Cherone left the band in 1999 because the rehearsals for their second album together did not go well.

- Before joining Van Halen, Sammy Hagar was the former frontman for a hard rock group known as Montrose.

- In 1985, Darryl Hall of Hall & Oates was offered the position of lead vocalist for Van Halen but declined.

- After leaving the band in 1996, Sammy Hagar returned to play with the band in 2004. The band's tour during this year was panned by the critics, mainly caused by a reputation for sloppy performances. However, it was commercially successful, netting the band $54.3 million. After Eddie smashed his guitar during the last show of the tour, the band entered a brief hiatus due to tensions between the members.

- In 2004, David Lee Roth began training to become a paramedic. He later received his Emergency Medical Technician certification for the state of New York.

- During Sammy Hagar's time with the band, fans often referred to it as "Van Hagar" instead of Van Halen, in order to differentiate from when David Lee Roth was the lead vocalist.

- Alex Van Halen, born in 1953, is two years older than his brother Eddie Van Halen, born in 1955.

- Former member Gary Cherone got his musical start in the band known as Extreme. Extreme was popular in the 1990s, and Cherone was a successful singer. In April 1992, Cherone performed with three members of the band Queen during The Freddie Mercury Tribute concert at Wembley Stadium.

- In addition to his music, Michael Anthony also has a business making hot sauces, called "Mad Anthony."

- After Roth departed the band, Sammy Hagar claimed that he knew Eddie Van Halen was going to call him. He said, "Who else were they going to get? There was Ozzy Osborne, Ronnie James Dio, and me."

- Before becoming an official member of Van Halen, Wolfgang Van Halen made several guest appearances during the band's performances, most often joining his father to play the song "316," named for Wolfgang's birthday.

- Wolfgang Van Halen has spoken about how during his childhood, he wasn't aware of his father's fame. He didn't realize Eddie was a famous musician until he saw pictures of him on album covers.

- Gary Cherone grew up in the city of Malden, Massachusetts. He is the third of five brothers, including his younger fraternal twin named Greg Cherone.

- Eddie Van Halen originally had a very shy and conservative personality. He suffered from extreme stage fright, and hated giving interviews or posing for photographs for the public. David Lee Roth was quite the opposite; his hyperactive personality allowed him to take some of the spotlight off of Eddie, as he was dubbed the "spokesperson" for the band.

- As a teenager, future Van Halen lead singer Sammy Hagar was obsessed with the rock bands of his time. At 17 years old, he snuck into the Swing Auditorium in San Bernardino to see the American debut of the Rolling Stones in 1964.

- In addition to being the bassist for Van Halen, Michael Anthony was also a backing vocalist.

- Sammy Hagar departed as lead vocalist in 1996. The exact cause of his separation from Van Halen is disputed, but many attribute it to interpersonal tensions between Hagar and the Van Halen brothers, as well as creative disagreements about an album compilation.

- During his youth, David Lee Roth was known for being a problematic teen. He was prone to fits of hyperactivity and was even sent to a horse ranch for "troubled teens" by his parents.

CHAPTER 4:

SOUNDS AND SONGS

TRIVIA TIME!

1. One of the first songs the Van Halen brothers performed during The Broken Combs era was…
   a. "Boogie Booger"
   b. "Rumpus"
   c. A and B
   d. "Leap"

2. Which song was Van Halen's first #1 in America?
   a. "Leap"
   b. "Jump"
   c. "Hop"
   d. "Skip"

3. Who receives credit and royalties for songwriting for Van Halen?
   a. Eddie Van Halen
   b. Eddie and Alex Van Halen
   c. All of the band members

d. The producers

4. In their first performances, what was unusual about the way Eddie Van Halen played guitar?

    a. He would play upside down
    b. He always smashed his guitar at the end
    c. Nothing, he played just like anyone else
    d. He would play with his back to the audience so no one would steal his sound

5. Eddie Van Halen played a guitar solo in which famous hit by another artist?

    a. "Beat It" by Michael Jackson
    b. "Smells Like Teen Spirit" by Nirvana
    c. "Johnny B. Goode" by Chuck Berry
    d. "Sharp Dressed Man" by ZZ Top

6. Van Halen's hit song "Jump" was released in which year?

    a. 1980
    b. 1984
    c. 1982
    d. 1986

7. Eddie's famous solo "Eruption" is featured on which album?

    a. Van Halen
    b. 5150
    c. Van Halen II
    d. Women and Children First

8. Eddie Van Halen did what to his guitars to ensure that they were "just right?"

    a. Never used the same guitar twice
    b. Bought specially made guitars from Japan
    c. Constantly took apart and rebuilt his own guitars
    d. All of the above

9. True or False: Although bassist Michael Anthony is left-handed, he plays the bass right-handed.

10. Eddie Van Halen attributes his success in songwriting to which of the following?
    a. Inspiration from his brother Alex
    b. His father Jan's teaching
    c. His study of classical music
    d. All of the above

11. True or False: David Lee Roth and producer Ted Templeman opposed Eddie recording the song "Jump," which would later become the lead single of *1984*.

12. Bassist Michael Anthony's former band, Snake, played covers from which music groups?
    a. ZZ Top
    b. Led Zeppelin
    c. Neither ZZ Top nor Led Zeppelin
    d. Both ZZ Top and Led Zeppelin

13. True or False: The band's first album, *Van Halen*, yielded their first top 20 single.

14. The song "Jump" features which instrument?
    a. A trumpet
    b. A synthesizer
    c. A keyboard
    d. A saxophone

15. Van Halen's song "Mean Street" is featured on which one of their albums?
    a. Women and Children First
    b. 5150
    c. Van Halen II
    d. Fair Warning

16. The *Women and Children First* album featured which two singles?
    a. "Hot for Teacher" and "Dance the Night Away"
    b. "And the Cradle will Rock..." and "Somebody Get Me a Doctor"
    c. "Panama" and "Eruption"
    d. "Unchained" and "Mean Street"

17. True or False: David Lee Roth and Eddie Van Halen had creative disagreements. Roth wanted to record darker and edgier songs, while Van Halen pushed for a more pop music style.

ANSWERS:

1. C
2. B
3. C
4. D
5. A
6. B
7. A
8. C
9. True
10. C
11. True
12. B
13. False
14. B
15. D
16. B
17. False. It was actually the opposite; Van Halen pushed for darker and edgier songs, while Roth wanted a more pop music style.

DID YOU KNOW?

- Even though all the band members received equal royalties and credit for songwriting, Eddie Van Halen wrote the music for most of the songs while David Lee Roth and Sammy Hagar composed the lyrics.

- When Eddie Van Halen recorded the guitar solo on the hit song "Beat It" by Michael Jackson, he did not receive any royalties or credit for it. Van Halen claims he recorded the solo as a courtesy to Jackson's producer, Quincy Jones. He also said he received payment in the form of beer.

- "Jump" was the second song that Van Halen recorded at 5150 Studios. The studio was built in 1983 by Eddie Van Halen so that he could have a more hands-on approach to recording the band's music.

- The hit song "Panama" is said to have been inspired by a car that David Lee Roth saw in a race in Las Vegas named "Panama Express." The song was the third single released in the album *1984*.

- The album *5150* is named for the police code that Van Halen's producer, Donn Landee, once heard on his police scanner. The four digits of the California Welfare & Institutions Code signals that a qualified police officer may put an involuntary psychiatric hold on a person if that person is displaying behavior that is "as a result of a mental disorder, a danger to themselves, a danger to others, or gravely disabled."

- Sections of the song "Jump" are said to have been written in the back of Van Halen's tour bus in 1981. The song was not released until 1984 because the band struggled to agree on where it belonged on their albums.

- When Van Halen first began releasing albums, rumors began to spread that the band was actually composed of the members of KISS, but without their outrageous stage makeup. The rumor is thought to have been started by the fact of Gene Simmons discovering the band, and because, when the band began recording songs in 1977, KISS had taken a hiatus.

- David Lee Roth claims that the song "Dance the Night Away" was written by him as a tribute to an intoxicated woman who was having intercourse in the back of a truck and ran from the police with her pants on backwards into the club where Van Halen was performing that night.

- The song "Hot for Teacher" was the last single released by Van Halen's original lineup of Eddie, Alex, Michael, and David. It was featured on the band's sixth studio album, *1984*.

- David Lee Roth wrote the lyric "Go ahead and jump," featured in the single "Jump." He was inspired to write the song after seeing a man on the news threatening to commit suicide on the Arco Tower in Los Angeles. Roth stated, "There's always one guy in the crowd who tells the guy to just jump."

- The ending of the song "Hot for Teacher" is from a studio outtake back when Van Halen only played in the LA club scene. The outtake is titled "Voodoo Queen."

- David Lee Roth wrote the song "Panama" after being accused of only writing songs about partying, beautiful women, and fast cars. Roth realized he had actually never written a song about fast cars, so he decided to take his inspiration from a car race to make the song.

- While Eddie Van Halen is not the creator of the finger-tapping technique, he is the one who officially named that style of playing.

- Van Halen's song "Poundcake" is known for featuring the sound of Eddie's Makita 6012HD power drill before and during Eddie's guitar solo.

- "Panama" is rumored to be the name of David Lee Roth's Opel Kadett, a German automobile produced from 1962 through 1991. The car was featured in Roth's music video for the song "SHOO Bop."

- Fans got a sneak peek of Van Halen's song "Jump" when Eddie played the ending of the song during the 1983 Us Festival after performing "Dance the Night Away."

- The band originally did not want "Dance the Night Away" to be their first released single. The quartet felt the song was more upbeat and lighter than the rest of their content, and did not want this song to become the "face" of their brand. Unfortunately, they did not have the standing to overrule the record company, and so "Dance the Night Away" was released in 1979 on the album *Van Halen II*.

- Van Halen's song "Hot for Teacher" features Alex Van Halen's 30-second double bass drum performance.

- During the bridge of the song "Panama," Eddie Van Halen can be heard revving the engine of his 1972 Lamborghini Miura S. To record the engine for the song, microphones had to be attached to the exhaust pipes.

- Eddie Van Halen's finger-tapping guitar technique was showcased in the instrumental song "Eruption." Alex Van Halen accompanies his brother in a short intro on the drums.

- Twenty years after the band began opening for Black Sabbath, the two bands co-wrote the song "Evil Eye." However, Eddie was not credited for the song for legal reasons.

- Eddie Van Halen actually rearranged some of the song "Beat It" without Michael Jackson's permission. After hearing the song, he began directing the sound engineer on where to move pieces of the song for a better fit. In the end, Jackson approved all the changes.

CHAPTER 5:

WILD PERFORMANCES

TRIVIA TIME!

1. In 2012, Van Halen played a miniature gig at which popular restaurant in Manhattan?
   a. Cafe Wha?
   b. Hard Rock Cafe
   c. Cafe Feenjon
   d. Cafe Au Go Go

2. Van Halen was classified as which type of act?
   a. "Guitar hero"
   b. "Disco"
   c. "Yacht rock"
   d. "New wave"

3. After Van Halen released their debut album, their first official tour was with which band?
   a. AC/DC
   b. Bon Jovi
   c. Black Sabbath

d. Journey

4. True or False: Van Halen's reputation suffered because, historically, its albums were better than their live performances.

5. During their tour in 1979, David Lee Roth would give Van Halen's roadies backstage passes to hand out to attractive women. If Roth "shacked up" with one of the women, the roadies would get which of the following rewards?
   a. Brought up onstage to perform with the band
   b. $100 cash
   c. Access to the band's personal chef
   d. A chance to meet members of the famous bands they toured with

6. Journey eventually grew tired of touring with Van Halen and even tried to kick them off as their opening act for which reason?
   a. Poor reviews of Van Halen after the shows
   b. The band's tendency to trash hotels and throw wild parties
   c. Making musical errors while onstage
   d. All of the above

7. The only way Eddie Van Halen could conquer his stage fright was by doing which of the following?
   a. Talking to his father before performing
   b. Having a few alcoholic drinks and a cigarette
   c. Rehearsing for hours right up until the show

d. Getting a pep talk from fellow member David Lee
   Roth

8. In 1978, the band performed which famous stunt?
   a. Setting a guitar on fire
   b. Using live fireworks onstage
   c. Parachuting onto the stage
   d. All of the above

9. While touring with Journey, Van Halen would blame their
   destruction of hotels on which group?
   a. Crazed fans
   b. The band Journey
   c. Hotel staff
   d. Teenagers who happened to be staying at the hotel

10. When writing contracts with venues and promoters for
    their performances, Van Halen would include which odd
    request?
    a. The dressing room doors be painted black
    b. To have a bowl of M&Ms with no brown ones
    c. A personal chef provide catering backstage
    d. Exactly four sound-checks to be completed before the
       show

11. True or False: The band often had sexual relations with
    random groupies and fans, which led to frequent trips to
    doctors for treatment of many different STDs.

12. During their tours in the early '80s, Eddie Van Halen used which drug to give him his signature "energy" while playing his guitar solos?

    a. Adderall
    b. Percocet
    c. Cocaine
    d. Crystal meth

13. Eddie Van Halen almost went onstage covered entirely in which of these things?

    a. Red paint
    b. Glitter
    c. Sharpie markings
    d. All of the above

14. According to Van Halen's manager, Noel Monk, Eddie once threw which of these at David Lee Roth?

    a. A guitar
    b. A sandwich
    c. A bowl of guacamole
    d. A book

15. During the band's Fair Warning tour, David Lee Roth had an outburst. The band members did which of the following to calm him down?

    a. Sang David's favorite song
    b. Made him drink a bottle of Scotch
    c. Put him in a straitjacket
    d. Locked him in a dressing room

16. When opening for the Rolling Stones, what did Mick Jagger do?
    a. Sabotaged the sound equipment
    b. Put brown M&Ms in the band's dressing room
    c. Punched Alex Van Halen
    d. Banned Eddie Van Halen's custom-made bombshell prop

17. While performing a one-off show for singer Ted Nugent, which of the following events happened?
    a. Nugent pushed bassist Michael Anthony offstage
    b. Eddie Van Halen broke Nugent's guitar
    c. The crowd cheered for Van Halen instead of Nugent
    d. All of the above

18. For the song "Poundcake," Eddie Van Halen performed with which prop?
    a. A cake
    b. A hammer
    c. A power drill
    d. A bombshell

19. What did the band Journey think after first seeing Van Halen play during their tour?
    a. They were unimpressed
    b. They were bored
    c. They were blown away
    d. They were jealous

ANSWERS:

1. A
2. A
3. D
4. False
5. B
6. B
7. B
8. C
9. B
10. B
11. True
12. C
13. C
14. C
15. C
16. D
17. C
18. C
19. C

DID YOU KNOW?

- The Guinness Book of World Records created a new category just for the band. In exchange for headlining at a festival in San Bernardino, California called "Heavy Metal Day," Van Halen charged the hefty fee of $1.5 million dollars. This became the single most expensive one-time appearance of a band.

- When Van Halen opened for Journey on their first tour, the members of Journey saw how well-received the band was by the crowd. The audience was so pumped up, Journey was afraid to be the following act.

- While on tour with Journey, the band learned that a venue in Madison, Wisconsin did not have the space for all three bands: Journey, Montrose, and Van Halen. Van Halen decided to book a smaller gig at a local club. Audience members say the performance was wild, and the club was "baptized with geysers of champagne."

- The rivalry between Van Halen and Journey while the bands toured together was intense. Journey tried to tamper with Van Halen's PA equipment, and Van Halen often stole food and women from Journey's backstage area.

- In 1978, Van Halen took a break from their world tour to perform a show at Long Beach Arena. The band sold out the 9,000-seat venue with ease and spent a whopping $20,000 on special effects.

- During the band's 2008 tour, David Lee Roth demanded that his dressing room have a floor covering so that he could practice martial arts.

- In 2004, the band staged an intervention for Eddie's wild behavior on and offstage, mainly fueled by his alcoholism. The meeting was not well received by Eddie, but eventually he and the rest of the band members agreed that he needed to clean up his act.

- One of the wildest Van Halen fiascos occurred on tour with Journey. The band stayed at the Sheraton Inn in Madison, Wisconsin and absolutely trashed the hotel, spraying fire extinguishers throughout the hallways and even throwing televisions out of windows.

- While touring with Black Sabbath in 1978, lead singer Ozzy Osborne was so in awe of Van Halen's opening performance that he tried to back out of the show entirely. He said, "We were just too stunned to speak."

- Eddie Van Halen met his wife, actress Valerie Bertinelli, when she brought her brother backstage to meet the band members.

- During their performance at Anaheim Stadium's Summerfest, the band famously "parachuted" onto the stage. The audience watched as four stuntmen, bearing a striking resemblance to the band members, landed in their jumpsuits, hopped in a van, and came onstage still wearing their jumpsuits. In reality the stuntmen completed the parachuting, while the true members of Van Halen had hidden in the van for hours before, drinking and playing games.

- The same night that Van Halen pulled their famous parachuting stunt, the band members met Sammy Hagar, who would replace lead singer David Lee Roth six years later.

- In 1978, Eddie Van Halen and David Lee Roth got into a heated argument backstage, and Eddie threw a bowl of guacamole at Roth. However, his aim was off and the guac landed on Steve Perry, the lead singer of Journey. Perry reportedly cried, although the singer denies it.

- Years of jumping up and down onstage during performances actually led Eddie Van Halen to need hip replacement surgery in 1999.

- When Van Halen played their first-ever show in New York City, the band was not met with the same enthusiasm from the audience that they would have in the future. The show was rampant with booing and heckling from the crowd. Several months later, however, when opening for Black Sabbath, the band earned the affection of the audience. Ozzy Osborne recalls thinking that his band should have been the opening act.

- Although David Lee Roth was known for flying and jumping around the stage, sometimes even diving into the audience to crowd-surf, he was actually terrified of heights and flying in an aircraft.

- Despite the band's antics, they were able to overcome any challenges they faced while performing. In 1978, upon returning from their tour in Japan to play at the Texxas Jam held in the Cotton Bowl stadium in Dallas, it became clear that all of their equipment had been set up at an incorrect venue in Chicago. Van Halen played with rented equipment in front of 82,000 people. The band recalls the show as being "one of the best."

CHAPTER 6:

TV AND MOVIES

TRIVIA TIME!

1. The earliest film to include music from Van Halen was which movie?
   a. The Breakfast Club (1985)
   b. The Outsiders (1983)
   c. Over the Edge (1979)
   d. *Porky's* (1981)

2. You can hear Van Halen in the movie score of which film?
   a. Back to the Future (1985)
   b. Suburbia (1983)
   c. The Lost Boys (1987)
   d. The Blue Lagoon (1980)

3. Eddie Van Halen has appeared on which television show?
   a. Two and a Half Men
   b. Friends
   c. It's Always Sunny in Philadelphia
   d. How I Met Your Mother

4. Which Van Halen song can be heard in the movie *Better Off Dead* (1985)?
   a. "Jump"
   b. "Dance the Night Away"
   c. "Everybody Wants Some!!"
   d. "Hot for Teacher"

5. True or False: Eddie Van Halen starred in a made-for-television version of *Footloose* (1984).

6. Recently, Van Halen's hit "Jump" was used in which 2018 film?
   a. Venom
   b. Ready Player One
   c. Suicide Squad
   d. A Star is Born

7. Which band member had a cameo on the popular sitcom *Frasier*?
   a. Michael Anthony
   b. David Lee Roth
   c. Alex Van Halen
   d. Eddie Van Halen

8. Which of these movies features the Van Halen song "Dance the Night Away"?
   a. Ocean's Eleven (2001)
   b. Sin City (2005)
   c. Mission to Mars (2000)
   d. The 40-year-old Virgin (2005)

9. In 1987, Eddie Van Halen co-hosted an episode of *Saturday Night Live* with which of the following people?

    a. David Lee Roth
    b. Wolfgang Van Halen
    c. Valerie Bertinelli
    d. Alex Van Halen

10. Van Halen songs were on the soundtrack of which movie?

    a. The Karate Kid (1984)
    b. Mystic Pizza (1988)
    c. National Lampoon's Vacation (1983)
    d. The Seduction of Gina (1983)

11. Which fake food played the song "Everybody Wants Some!!" in the film *Better off Dead* (1985)?

    a. A hotdog
    b. A salad
    c. A corncob
    d. A hamburger

12. True or False: Van Halen contributed to the soundtrack for the movie *Twister* (1996).

13. Eddie Van Halen had a cameo alongside his then-wife, actress Valerie Bertinelli, in which sitcom?

    a. Who's the Boss?
    b. Full House
    c. Cafe Americain

d. Cheers

14. *Lethal Weapon 4* (1998) features which of the band's songs?
    a. "Jump"
    b. "Good Enough"
    c. "And the Cradle Will Rock…"
    d. "Fire in the Hole"

15. In 2020, Van Halen's song "Panama" was featured in which adult cartoon?
    a. BoJack Horseman
    b. Family Guy
    c. South Park
    d. Bob's Burgers

16. Which song by Sammy Hagar was featured in *Footloose* (1984)?
    a. "Heavy Metal"
    b. "Your Love is Driving Me Crazy"
    c. "The Girl Gets Around"
    d. "I'll Fall in Love Again"

17. David Lee Roth had a cameo in which 2019 movie?
    a. The Dirt
    b. Uncut Gems
    c. Ford vs. Ferrari
    d. Dolemite is My Name

18. Van Halen's hit song "Jump" is in which film?
    a. Help Wanted: Kids (1986)
    b. Big Daddy (1999)

c. Herbie: Fully Loaded (2005)

d. All of the above

19. True or False: Eddie and Alex Van Halen wrote and directed a biographical movie about the band that never came to fruition.

20. David Lee Roth had a cameo in which of the following television shows?

a. The Wire

b. Ozark

c. The Sopranos

d. Dexter

ANSWERS:

1. C

2. A

3. A

4. C

5. False

6. B

7. D

8. C

9. C

10. D

11. D

12. True

13. C

14. D

15. B

16. C

17. A

18. D

19. False

20. C

DID YOU KNOW?

- The 1996 film *Twister* was an action and romance blockbuster film that became one of the most popular movies of the '90s. Van Halen contributed an original song created especially for the movie, entitled "Humans Being."

- In the 1960s, the famous British-American comedian Bob Hope created his own golf tournament, an event first known as the Palm Springs Golf Classic. It was for this event that Hope would invite popular figures and celebrities to play alongside professionals in the sport. In 1994, professional golfer Tom Kite played with Hope, President Gerald Ford, and Eddie Van Halen.

- In 2018, Steven Spielberg's film *Ready Player One* featured Van Halen's song "Jump" in the film's first released trailer. Based on the novel by Ernest Cline, the movie is set in a dystopian future in which people compete in a virtual reality competition.

- The 1970s sitcom *WKRP In Cincinnati* was the first television show to feature Van Halen's music. The band's album *Van Halen* was only months old when the show featured their song "Atomic Punk."

- The Van Halen song "Panama" was featured in a notorious scene in the popular film *Superbad* (2007). Actor

Bill Hader originally sang the song as improv, and the director liked it so much he added it to the film.

- When American media personality Howard Stern took his radio show *The Howard Stern Show* to Sirius satellite radio, terrestrial radio was left with a large gap in its programming. David Lee Roth was asked to replace Stern and his show, and so, in 2006, *The David Lee Roth Show* began airing on the radio.

- When he had his guest appearance on the TV show *Two and a Half Men*, Eddie Van Halen performed a number titled "Two Burritos and a Root Beer Float." The riff from this song was also incorporated into Van Halen's official song "As Is," written about the Opel Kadett car that David Lee Roth used to own.

- In 1996, the band was taking a break after just finishing The Balance "Ambulance" Tour in November 1995. Van Halen's manager approached Alex and Eddie about writing a song for the movie *Twister*. At first, all of the members were reluctant to do so. Eddie was on painkillers following recovery from a hip injury resulting from a case of avascular necrosis. Meanwhile, Alex was using a neck brace for a vertebrae injury and Sammy Hagar was expecting the birth of his child soon. Eventually, they considered the financial benefits and wrote the song.

- The 2000 film *Mission to Mars* features the song "Dance the Night Away" from the album *Van Halen II*. The song is used in a scene where two astronauts dance together in zero gravity.

- *The Seduction of Gina* (1984) was a made-for-TV film that Eddie Van Halen's wife, Valerie Bertinelli, starred in. Van Halen composed the score for the movie alongside Tom Neuman.

- On playing golf with Bob Hope, Eddie Van Halen said, "I met Bob Hope over at Lakeside Country Club (in Toluca Lake) about six months ago and he asked me if I wanted to play... I had no idea I would be playing with Bob. And President Ford. And Tom Kite." Bob Hope's competition had a reputation for being filled with more conservative celebrities, so the left-leaning Eddie Van Halen was a sort of outlier. This was done on purpose by Hope in an attempt to draw a bigger crowd to his event.

- For *The Seduction of Gina* (1984), Eddie Van Halen wrote three songs for the movie. Each song incorporated a synthesizer. He wrote the first song without ever seeing any footage of the film. After the director heard Eddie's work, he was asked to complete the score for the film.

- In the PlayStation 2 game *Guitar Hero*, you can play several Van Halen songs and rock out as a member of the band.

- Eddie Van Halen was one of the first celebrities who agreed to be a guest caller on the sitcom *Frasier*. He took the role as a favor to star Kelsey Grammar, with whom the guitarist was friends. Van Halen played a caller named Hank who claimed he had difficulty hearing the main character Frasier on his radio show.

- On making a guest appearance in *The Sopranos*, David Lee Roth said, "Mom says I'm going to look like Lee Marvin in ten years whether I'm in the movies or not, so I might as well get after it!"

- The movie *Back to the Future* (1985) features a scene where Marty McFly puts on a spacesuit and slips a cassette into his Walkman, placing his headphones over the ears of his father in order to wake him up and get his attention. Loud guitar work can be heard during this scene, and for years there were rumors that the guitar was recorded by Eddie Van Halen. In 2012, Van Halen confirmed to TMZ that the work was indeed his.

- Van Halen's song "Dance the Night Away" was featured in the 2012 movie *Argo*.

- When writing the song for the film *Twister*, Alex Van Halen originally wrote the lyrics to reflect the content of the extreme weather featured in the movie. The directors asked if the song could be unrelated to the tornadoes, so the lyrics were changed to be about falling in love with a woman who "sucks you in."

- A poster of Sammy Hagar performing before he joined Van Halen can be seen in the sitcom *WKRP In Cincinnati*.

- The popular science fiction comedy *Spaceballs*, released in 1987, features the Van Halen song "Good Enough."

CHAPTER 7:

THE GOOD, THE BAD, THE UGLY

TRIVIA TIME!

1. Who was Van Halen's original bass player?
   a. Michael Anthony
   b. Mark Stone
   c. Jan Van Halen
   d. None of the above

2. One of the first disagreements between the Van Halen brothers and David Lee Roth was over which of these issues?
   a. The record company that was signing them
   b. Who was writing the songs
   c. The name of the band
   d. Who was receiving the most royalties

3. Mark Stone left Mammoth in which year?
   a. 1972
   b. 1974
   c. 1976

d. 1980

4. Eddie Van Halen and David Lee Roth began to have pronounced differences in artistic vision during the recording of which album?
    a. Van Halen
    b. Van Halen II
    c. Fair Warning
    d. 1984

5. MTV banned which of Van Halen's music videos?
    a. "Hot for Teacher"
    b. "(Oh) Pretty Woman"
    c. "Dance the Night Away"
    d. "And the Cradle Will Rock..."

6. What happened during the show that earned Van Halen the Guinness World Record for the highest-paid single appearance ever?
    a. Eddie did not play with the band
    b. David Lee Roth was high and forgot the lyrics
    c. The band played their most unpopular songs
    d. The band was three hours late to the performance

7. David Lee Roth decided to leave the band in which year?
    a. 1986
    b. 1980
    c. 1985
    d. 1982

8. Van Halen got into a famous fight with which other band?

a. Journey

b. AC/DC

c. Mötley Crüe

d. KISS

9. Eddie Van Halen threw a bowl of guacamole at David Lee Roth to get back at him for doing which of these?

    a. Insulting his singing before the performance

    b. Threatening to leave the band

    c. Throwing peanuts at Eddie

    d. Stealing his girlfriend

10. True or False: Eddie Van Halen faced a paternity lawsuit that was eventually dismissed.

11. Eddie Van Halen struggled with an addiction to which of the following?

    a. Opioids

    b. Alcohol

    c. Gambling

    d. Heroin

12. Which of these contributed to Sammy Hagar leaving the band in 1996?

    a. He wanted to join David Lee Roth's band

    b. He wanted all of the songwriting credit

    c. He and Michael Anthony were going to start their own band

d. He and the band had disagreements over their song for the movie *Twister* (1996)

13. True or False: Gary Cherone left the band in 2004 due to musical differences with the band.

14. Van Halen's reunion with Sammy Hagar was during the release of which album?
    a. Van Halen III
    b. Pasadena 1977
    c. Best of Both Worlds
    d. A Different Kind of Truth

15. Which problem fueled most of the tension between the members of Van Halen from 2000 and on?
    a. Lack of monetary success
    b. Eddie's addiction
    c. Constant search for a better lead vocalist
    d. All of the above

16. Van Halen officially disbanded in 2020 due to which event?
    a. Sammy Hagar leaving the band again
    b. Alex Van Halen going to rehab
    c. Too many disagreements between all of the members
    d. Eddie Van Halen's death

ANSWERS:

1. A
2. C
3. B
4. C
5. B
6. B
7. C
8. C
9. C
10. True
11. B
12. D
13. False
14. B
15. B
16. D

DID YOU KNOW?

- In 1998, David Lee Roth published his autobiography, *Crazy from the Heat*. Roth describes his initial breakup from the band as being sudden and "morose."

- The members of Van Halen and the rock band Mötley Crüe got into a fight during a dinner in Sweden, where the members of AC/DC were also in attendance.

- In 1980, a woman in San Diego filed a paternity lawsuit against Eddie Van Halen. Van Halen claimed that their relationship was limited to the "front seat of his car" and that they'd never had intercourse. After telling his bride-to-be Valerie Bertinelli about the suit, he agreed to take the paternity test, and the suit was dismissed.

- The original line-up of the band reunited shortly the year after Sammy Hagar departed from Van Halen in 1995.

- American music manager Doc McGhee said that of all of the rock bands he encountered, Mötley Crüe was more like a gang than a band, often on drugs and exhibiting their own strange behaviors. This pattern led to the fight with the members of Van Halen.

- Even after the band had "reunited" with Roth in 1996, Eddie and Alex Van Halen were still auditioning other lead vocalists. Among these was singer Mitch Malloy.

- One of the biggest factors for why Sammy Hagar departed from Van Halen was that his wife was expected to give birth at the same time the band was working on the music for the movie *Twister*.

- David Lee Roth started his solo career before he had officially left Van Halen. Creative differences with Eddie Van Halen, and getting an offer from CBS Pictures for a film deal for *Crazy from the Heat*, were the final two straws that pushed Roth out.

- One of the main reasons that Eddie Van Halen built his own studio, known as 5150 Studios in Los Angeles, was so he would have more control over the songs the band recorded, as well as bypass the compromises he was forced to make with David Lee Roth.

- Mötley Crüe bassist Nikki Sixx revealed that their falling-out with Van Halen was because, while on tour with the band in Sweden, lead singer Vince Neil bit Eddie Van Halen on the hand. This led to an enormous fight, which almost resulted in Mötley Crüe being kicked off the tour.

- Eddie Van Halen's addiction unfortunately took a large toll on everyone around him. During his wedding, after he and Valerie Bertinelli exchanged their vows, former manager Noel Monk recalls trying to locate the couple, as they had vanished before the reception. He found them in an upstairs bathroom with Valerie holding Eddie's hair back as he vomited from alcohol poisoning, with tears streaming down her face.

- After Eddie Van Halen faced a paternity suit, David Lee Roth got the idea to protect himself from the same possible issue. Unfortunately, no insurance company would provide such coverage.

- Eddie's addiction and drug consumption worsened as Van Halen's fame rose. With money and resources, he was given access to a personal drug dealer who provided him with the highest quality Peruvian cocaine.

- One of the larger disagreements Eddie Van Halen and David Lee Roth had was specifically over their released cover of the song "Dancing in the Street." Van Halen wanted the song to be "more like a Peter Gabriel song than what it turned out to be," while Roth and producer Ted Templeman wanted the song to remain more classic in the pop/rock genre.

- When musicians are given awards and recognized at the MTV Music Awards, it is customary for presenters to stand quietly as they accept the award. Roth, however, would dance around crazily, doing everything he possibly could to be the center of attention. Van Halen was horrified and embarrassed by his behavior.

- Alex Van Halen also struggled with alcohol abuse. He would become so intoxicated that he would have delusions and bouts of psychosis.

- After Van Halen's first tour, they owed Warner Bros. close to $1 million despite the tour's success. The band's antics — trashing hotels, stages, and limos — was so intense that the band was left with more debt than monetary success.

- When speaking on his creative differences with David Lee Roth and producer Ted Templeman, Eddie Van Halen said, "My philosophy has always been that I would rather bomb with my own music than make it with other people's music." In the end, Eddie admitted that he wanted more control over Van Halen's content because he did not feel that the music they were making was his.

- As the band rose to success, bassist Michael Anthony was pushed to the outskirts of the band. He did not imbibe nearly as much drugs and alcohol as the rest of the band and began to be on the outside as the other members fell deeper into intoxication-fueled tension and fighting. Eventually, Anthony's exclusion became so extreme that Van Halen decided to strip him of songwriting royalties, and Anthony lost millions of dollars.

- Former manager Noel Monk said that despite working with Van Halen for over seven years, endlessly renegotiating contracts for the band and earning them millions, the band never offered him a permanent contract. After Monk finished working for them, he says Van Halen never spoke to him again.

- Touring with Gary Cherone as the lead singer for Van Halen yielded minor success. In the end, Cherone left the band. This breakup was one of the few amicable ones the band experienced, and the members stayed in touch with Cherone and remained friends.

- After rumors of another reunion in 2007 at the induction ceremony for the band into the Rock and Roll Hall of Fame, David Lee Roth opted not to attend the ceremony. It is thought that this was because of a dispute over which songs the band would perform during the awards ceremony.

CHAPTER 8:

THE RECORDS THAT BROKE RECORDS

TRIVIA TIME!

1. How many copies had Van Halen's debut album, entitled *Van Halen* and released in 1978, sold by 1996?
   a. 20 million
   b. 1 million
   c. 10 million
   d. 5 million

2. As of 2019, how many albums had Van Halen sold worldwide?
   a. 50 million
   b. 80 million
   c. 100 million
   d. 150 million

3. True or False: As of 2019, Van Halen is one of only six rock groups to have two different albums sell over 10 million records in the United States.

4. Van Halen's first album reached which number on the *Billboard* charts?
    a. No. 1
    b. No. 19
    c. No. 6
    d. No. 4

5. The band's first top 20 single, "Dance the Night Away," reached which number on the *Billboard* Top 100?
    a. No. 5
    b. No. 15
    c. No. 10
    d. No. 8

6. True or False: None of Van Halen's album sales were inflated by payola, a popular practice in the industry to increase a song's popularity.

7. Van Halen's first album to reach No. 1 on the *Billboard* charts was entitled...
    a. Van Halen
    b. Van Halen II
    c. 1984
    d. 5150

8. In 1992, the band received which Grammy award?
    a. "Best Rock Performance"

b. "Best Performance by a Vocal Group"

c. "Best Hard Rock Performance with Vocal"

d. "Best Hard Rock Album"

9. The *Fair Warning* album reached which status?
   a. Double Gold
   b. Double Diamond
   c. Double Platinum
   d. Double Silver

10. True or False: VH-1 ranked Van Halen No. 1 on a list of the Top 100 Rock Artists of All Time.

11. Which song by Van Halen earned the Award for Best Stage Performance at the MTV Video and Music Awards in 1984?
    a. "Dance the Night Away"
    b. "Jump"
    c. "Everybody Wants Some!!"
    d. "5150"

12. Van Halen's album *1984* went platinum how many times?
    a. Four
    b. Three
    c. Two
    d. Five

13. The band's song "Panama" reached which number on the *Billboard* charts?
    a. No. 10
    b. No. 13

c. No. 15

d. No. 1

14. True or False: Van Halen did not initially enjoy financial success because their original deal with Warner Bros. Records paid them only $1 per album sold.

15. Which event helped Van Halen's compilation album *Best Of – Volume 1* reach No. 1 on the US album chart?
    a. Sammy Hagar leaving the band
    b. The reunion performance with David Lee Roth
    c. Eddie Van Halen going to rehab
    d. All of the above

16. How many of Van Halen's songs have charted No. 1 in the US throughout their career?
    a. 10
    b. 5
    c. 11
    d. 13

17. Van Halen's album *1984* included how many songs that became top 40 hits?
    a. Two
    b. Four
    c. One
    d. Five

18. True or False: Van Halen is tied for the most platinum albums released by an American band.

ANSWERS:

1. C
2. B
3. True
4. B
5. B
6. False
7. D
8. C
9. C
10. False
11. B
12. D
13. B
14. False
15. B
16. D
17. B
18. False

DID YOU KNOW?

- The band has sold over 56 million records in the United States alone.

- Van Halen's debut album, *Van Halen*, eventually sold over ten million copies in the US.

- After their first album's release, Van Halen went on tour with Black Sabbath for nine months. They returned in late 1978 and spent two weeks recording their second album, *Van Halen II*, which included their first hit single, "Dance the Night Away."

- Part of the reason Eddie Van Halen was so eager for Sammy Hagar to join the band after David Lee Roth's departure was because of Hagar's emerging success. He was formerly a member of the band Montrose and had left to begin a solo career. The previous year he had released the hit single "I Can't Drive 55," which appeared on his eighth studio album. The song was frequently played during Van Halen shows as the band went on tour.

- Van Halen's album *1984* was one of the most well-received albums the band produced. It peaked at No. 2 on the Billboard charts, just behind Michael Jackson's *Thriller*.

- The band recorded a remake of the Roy Orbison song, "Oh, Pretty Woman," entitled "(Oh) Pretty Woman." The remake reached No. 12 on the Billboard charts and was paired with a music video that increased its popularity, despite the fact that MTV banned it.

- Van Halen's album *Fair Warning* initially did not sell as well as its predecessors. However, it eventually reached platinum status, partially thanks to a $250,000 boost through payola. Payola is the practice of paying a commercial radio station to play a song and the radio broadcasting the song without making it public that the station was paid. It is considered illegal under United States law.

- In 1986, Van Halen released their first album with Sammy Hagar as lead vocalist, entitled *5150*. This was the band's first No. 1 album, and it included three top 40 singles: "Why Can't This Be Love," "Dreams," and "Love Walks In."

- As of today, Van Halen's albums Van Halen II, Women and Children First, Fair Warning, Diver Down, 5150, OU812, For Unlawful Carnal Knowledge and Balance have all achieved certified multi-platinum status.

- Van Halen is listed 20th on the Recording Industry Association of America's list of best-selling musical artists in the United States.

- At the 34th annual Grammy Awards, Van Halen received the Best Hard Rock Performance award in recognition of their For Unlawful Carnal Knowledge tour. The tour ran from 1991 to 1992, consisting of 99 separate dates. It was on this tour that the band recorded their live album, *Live: Right Here Right Now*. The VHS version of this album was also recorded on the tour.

- When the band was inducted into the Rock and Roll Hall of Fame, Alex and Eddie Van Halen, David Lee Roth, Sammy Hagar, and Michael Anthony were inducted. Only Hagar and Anthony attended the official ceremony.

- After lead vocalist Sammy Hagar left the band in 1996, they reunited in 2004 to record the compilation album *The Best of Both Worlds*, which included three new original songs with Hagar. The band then went on tour in the summer of that year and grossed a total of $55 million. This tour, dubbed the Summer of 2004 Tour, was one of the top ten grossing tours of 2004.

- Van Halen's single "Right Now," released in 1992, received three awards at the 1992 MTV Video Music Awards, including Video of the Year. They were nominated for four further awards that year.

- During the 1980s, Van Halen and another popular rock band, Heart, both had 15 *Billboard* Top 100 hits, which was more than any other rock or heavy metal band before them.

- *Van Halen III*, released in 1998, is regarded as the band's least commercially successful album. With Gary Cherone replacing Sammy Hagar as the lead vocalist, the album only earned a Gold certification, even though it reached No. 4 on the United States charts.

- The band's latest release, *A Different Kind of Truth*, debuted in 2012 and reached No. 2 on *Billboard*'s Top 200 Albums chart. The album sold almost 200,000 copies within the first week of its release, and it became the band's most popular album in the UK, debuting at No. 6.

- During their spat with Sammy Hagar, which eventually led to his departure from Van Halen, Alex and Eddie Van Halen alone recorded the instrumental song "Respect the Wind." This was the final song the band contributed to the 1996 movie *Twister*, as Hagar left before officially finishing the project. The Van Halen brothers' performance of the song earned them the Grammy nomination for Best Rock Instrumental Performance at the 39th Annual Grammy Awards.

- The four albums released during the time Sammy Hagar was with the band from 1986-1996 all reached No. 1 on the Billboard charts.

- David Lee Roth's solo career was started by two hit singles, both of which were cover songs. Roth remade The Beach Boys song "California Girls," which reached #3 on the US charts, and recorded a song combining "Just a

Gigolo" by Irving Caesar and "I Ain't Got Nobody" by Spencer Williams, which reached #12.

- Van Halen's first album, entitled *Van Halen*, did not yield any top 20 singles, but reached No. 19 on *Billboard*'s Pop Music charts. It is considered one of the most commercially successful debut albums to this day.

CHAPTER 9:

EVERYONE GETS THE SPOTLIGHT

TRIVIA TIME!

1. David Lee Roth left the band for which reason?
    a. Artistic differences with Eddie Van Halen
    b. Control over the band's "sound"
    c. A movie contract
    d. All of the above

2. In the band's 1998 album, *Van Halen III*, bassist Michael Anthony only played on how many songs?
    a. Five
    b. Three
    c. Two
    d. None

3. Eddie Van Halen made a cameo appearance in which music video?
    a. Michael Jackson's "Thriller"
    b. Black Sabbath's "Iron Man"
    c. Frank Sinatra's "L.A. is My Lady"

d. Bon Jovi's "You Give Love a Bad Name"

4. David Lee Roth's first solo album was titled which of the following?
   a. Eat 'Em and Smile
   b. Crazy from the Heat
   c. Just Like Paradise
   d. Skyscraper

5. Michael Anthony was fired from the band in which year?
   a. 1996
   b. 1998
   c. 2000
   d. 2006

6. True or False: Sammy Hagar enjoyed the peak of his solo career before joining Van Halen.

7. Eddie Van Halen was awarded patents for which of these items?
   a. Folding prop for a guitar
   b. Tension adjusting tailpiece
   c. Ornamental design for a headstock
   d. Guitar support system

8. After leaving the band, Michael Anthony made appearances on the solo tour for which artist?
   a. Alex Van Halen
   b. David Lee Roth
   c. Sammy Hagar
   d. Gary Cherone

9. David Lee Roth's least commercially successful album was titled which of the following?
   a. A Little Ain't Enough
   b. Cliffhanger
   c. Skyscraper
   d. Diamond Dave

10. What was the name of the band Sammy Hagar occasionally played with after leaving Van Halen for the first time?
    a. Montrose
    b. Snake
    c. Los Tres Gusanos
    d. Van Hagar

11. In which year did Michael Anthony form the band Planet Us?
    a. 2000
    b. 2004
    c. 2002
    d. 2006

12. David Lee Roth's album *Eat 'Em and Smile* sold how many copies?
    a. 500,000
    b. 1 million
    c. 1.5 million
    d. 2 million

13. The solo record Sammy Hagar recorded in 1997 that hit #1 on the Mainstream Rock Tracks chart was titled...

    a. Psycho Vertigo
    b. Marching to Mars
    c. Peephole
    d. Space Between

14. Which other member of Van Halen played with Michael Anthony in the band Planet Us?
    a. David Lee Roth
    b. Gary Cherone
    c. Sammy Hagar
    d. Alex Van Halen

15. For which song did Eddie Van Halen play the guitar solo that earned him the #2 spot on *Guitar World*'s poll of "100 Greatest Guitar Solos"?
    a. "Eruption"
    b. "Respect the Wind"
    c. "Little Guitars"
    d. "Dreams"

16. In 1995, David Lee Roth played some club gigs with members of which band?
    a. The Red Hot Chili Peppers
    b. Bon Jovi
    c. Miami Sound Machine
    d. None of the above

17. Eddie Van Halen's first recorded keyboard work is on which song?

a. "Eruption"
b. "And the Cradle Will Rock…"
c. "Dreams"
d. "When It's Love"

18. Sammy Hagar's reunion with Van Halen on tour in 2004 ended poorly because Eddie did which of these?
    a. Pushed Hagar off of the stage
    b. Smashed his guitar
    c. Got drunk before the show and forgot the song lyrics
    d. Threw up on an audience member

19. True or False: Sammy Hagar refused to play in the reunion tour unless Gary Cherone was invited to join them.

20. What is the name of the song co-written by David Lee Roth and guitarist Steve Vai?
    a. "Song of Love"
    b. "Slam Dunk"
    c. "Yankee Rose"
    d. None of the above

ANSWERS:

1. D

2. B

3. C

4. A

5. D

6. True

7. D

8. C

9. D

10. C

11. C

12. D

13. B

14. C

15. A

16. C

17. B

18. B

19. False

20. B

DID YOU KNOW?

- Before David Lee Roth had even left Van Halen in 1985, he assembled his own band. The members included himself as lead vocalist, guitarist Steve Vai, bassist Billy Sheehan, and drummer Gregg Bissonette.

- During the same period, right before David Lee Roth left the band, Eddie Van Halen contributed songs to the musical score for the movie *The Wild Life* (1984).

- Beginning in 1996, rumors would occasionally circulate that Michael Anthony had been fired from Van Halen. The band claimed that he had not been fired, and Anthony continued to be a member until his official departure in 2006.

- In 1999, a few years after leaving Van Halen, Sammy Hagar went on to form the band known as The Waboritas. Members included Hagar as lead vocalist, Jesse Harms on the keyboard, guitarist Vic Johnson, and bassist Mona Gnader.

- Most of Eddie Van Halen's work outside of the band was contributing to and fully scoring movie and film soundtracks. Some of the films he worked on include the *Seduction of Gina* (1984), *Sacred Sin* (2006), and, as previously mentioned, *The Wild Life* (1984).

- During the summer of 2002, Sammy Hagar and David Lee Roth joined forces to go on the Song for Song, The Heavyweight Champs of Rock and Roll Tour. The tour was an overall success, mainly because fans had never expected that the two former members of Van Halen would ever get together.

- Van Halen's compilation album, *Best of Both Worlds*, was released in 2004. Michael Anthony did not play for or write the three new songs that were included. Even though he received no recognition for those three tracks, Anthony did sing backup vocals for all of the songs.

- The Skyscraper Tour was David Lee Roth's second solo tour. The tour was known for including major special effects, including Roth surfing on a surfboard above the rafters, then being lowered onto the stage. Parts of tour were filmed and included in Roth's music video for his song "Just Like Paradise."

- While Sammy Hagar and David Lee Roth were on tour together, former Van Halen singer Gary Cherone occasionally made appearances and played in their shows.

- One of Eddie Van Halen's larger projects separate from the band was donating 75 guitars he personally owned. He donated them all to the Mr. Holland's Opus Foundation, a charity whose focus is supporting musical programs in financially struggling schools.

- David Lee Roth's bestselling autobiography *Crazy from Heat* was written as a collection of over 1,200 monologues by Roth. The book was transcribed by a fan of Roth's, who was a Princeton graduate.

- David Lee Roth's first single on his first solo album was entitled "Yankee Rose." The song was featured in the videogame *Grand Theft Auto: Vice City*, which was released in 2002.

- After touring with Sammy Hagar, Michael Anthony started a new band known as Chickenfoot. Members of the band included bassist Anthony, lead vocalist Sammy Hagar, guitarist Joe Satriani, and The Red Hot Chili Peppers drummer Chad Smith. The band released its first album, entitled *Chickenfoot*, on June 4, 2009.

- In 1999, David Lee Roth wrote and recorded "Song of Love" for Ashley Abernathy, a nine-year-old girl who suffered from leukemia.

- Michael Anthony and Sammy Hagar's band Planet Us wrote and recorded a song titled "Psycho Vertigo." The song was originally written to be featured in the *Spider-Man* (2002) movie soundtrack, but ultimately did not make its way into the film.

- Despite still technically being a member of Chickenfoot, Sammy Hagar formed a different musical group in 2014 called Sammy Hagar and the Circle. Hagar commented on the name, saying it was his career "coming to a full circle."

- One of David Lee Roth's notable performances during his solo career was the Boston Pops Orchestra's event "Pop Goes the Fourth." The performance was broadcast live on television and had millions of viewers.

- Sammy Hagar's new band, Sammy Hagar and the Circle, released its first album in 2019. It reached No. 4 on the *Billboard* 200 chart, and No. 1 on *Billboard*'s Top Album Sales chart.

CHAPTER 10:

VAN HALEN TODAY

TRIVIA TIME!

1. Gary Cherone left the band in 1999 and did which of the
   following afterwards?
   a. Quit music completely
   b. Joined David Lee Roth's band
   c. Went on tour with a new band
   d. Continued writing songs for Van Halen

2. In 2003, who reported that the Van Halen brothers were
   once again working with Sammy Hagar?
   a. TMZ
   b. The Van Halen News Desk
   c. Eddie Van Halen
   d. Sammy Hagar

3. What did Sammy Hagar do after the release of this album?
   a. Quit the band again
   b. Went on tour with Van Halen
   c. Left to focus on his own band

d. Was injured and could not perform

4. True or False: Tension arose between the Van Halen brothers, Sammy Hagar, and Michael Anthony over Hagar and Anthony's commercial ventures outside the band. These included Anthony's hot sauce and Hagar's other band.

5. In 2006, David Lee Roth was featured in three songs of a Van Halen country tribute album entitled which of the following?
   a. Best of Both Worlds
   b. Best of—Volume I
   c. Strummin' with the Devil
   d. A Different Kind of Truth

6. In the summer of 2006, which two Van Halen members went on a tour known as The Other Half together?
   a. Eddie and Wolfgang Van Halen
   b. Sammy Hagar and Michael Anthony
   c. David Lee Roth and Sammy Hagar
   d. Eddie and Alex Van Halen

7. How much money did the 2007-2008 reunion tour with David Lee Roth gross?
   a. $50 million
   b. $93 million
   c. $78 million
   d. $68 million

8. True or False: Sammy Hagar opened his own restaurant in 2004.

9. When Van Halen went on tour in 2008, the band was plagued with rumors about which event?
    a. David Lee Roth leaving the band again
    b. Sammy Hagar suing Eddie Van Halen
    c. Eddie Van Halen being admitted into rehab
    d. Wolfgang Van Halen being arrested for drug possession

10. In 2016, Sammy Hagar began filming his own television show entitled which of the following?
    a. The Sammy Hagar Show
    b. Rock & Roll Road trip with Sammy Hagar
    c. Life of Hagar
    d. Rockin' with Sammy Hagar

11. David Lee Roth began a video webcast in 2012 on which platform?
    a. Discovery Channel
    b. Facebook
    c. YouTube
    d. AMC Network

12. Van Halen's last top 100 single is titled which of these?
    a. "Tattoo"
    b. "A Different Kind of Truth"
    c. "New Age"
    d. None of the above

13. The last year Van Halen produced original content was…
    a. 2008
    b. 2012
    c. 2010
    d. 2009

14. True or False: David Lee Roth was married during the band's 2007 reunion tour.

15. Van Halen was officially disbanded in which year?
    a. 2016
    b. 2019
    c. 2020
    d. 2018

ANSWERS:

1. C
2. B
3. B
4. True
5. C
6. B
7. B
8. True
9. C
10. B
11. C
12. A
13. B
14. False
15. C

DID YOU KNOW?

- Following Gary Cherone's departure from Van Halen and Eddie Van Halen recovering from hip surgery, the band went on a hiatus from 1999 to 2003, and did not release any content or official statements during that time.

- After he left the band, Gary Cherone joined a new band known as The Tribe of Judah. One of the songs he wrote for Van Halen, titled "Left for Dead," was scrapped and not included in Van Halen's discography, so Cherone used it on the album *The Tribe of Judah*.

- During summer 2006, Michael Anthony and Sammy Hagar began their own tour. The duo referred to it as The Other Half, a nod to them being "half" of Van Halen.

- Sammy Hagar pursued other commercial projects outside of Van Halen in the mid-2000s. His success in business began while he was still in the band when he opened his own nightclub in Cabo San Lucas, Mexico, known as Cabo Wabo Cantina. He began to distribute his own line of tequila at his club, similarly dubbed Cabo Wabo Tequila. In 2007, his brand became the second best-selling premium tequila in the United States.

- At the start of 2007, Van Halen officially announced that the band would be undertaking a 40-date North

American tour alongside former member David Lee Roth. They ended up playing 74 shows.

- During The Other Half tour, Michael Anthony and Sammy Hagar played Van Halen songs from when both David Lee Roth and Hagar were the lead vocalists.

- Sammy Hagar opened one of his own restaurants, Sammy's Beach Bar & Grill, in 2009. Located at a casino in St. Louis, the restaurant was successful enough that another was opened in a Southwest Airlines terminal in Las Vegas.

- In 2005, Eddie Van Halen's wife Valerie Bertinelli filed for divorce after the couple had been separated for over four years. They divorced two years later. In 2009, Van Halen married Janie Liszewski, the band's publicist.

- Van Halen's most recent album with new content was released in 2012. Entitled *A Different Kind of Truth*, the album was released with David Lee Roth as the lead vocalist, and the band went on tour the following month.

- After spending a total of almost 300 hours being tattooed when David Lee Roth lived in Japan, he created a skincare line in 2018 specifically for the care of tattooed skin. The line was named INK the Original.

- During the band's 2012 tour, several of the dates were postponed after Eddie Van Halen underwent surgery for a severe case of diverticulitis.

- Sammy Hagar began broadcasting his own radio show, called *Sammy Hagar's Top Rock Countdown*, in 2015. The show was mostly comprised of Hagar compiling multi-genre playlists of his favorite songs.

- Eddie Van Halen's son, Wolfgang Van Halen, joined the band in 2006 to replace bassist Michael Anthony. At 15 years old, he was the youngest-ever member of the band. He played alongside his father during the band's 2007-2008 tour and returned to school the following year. He graduated in 2010.

- Outside of music, David Lee Roth is a certified emergency medical technician (EMT) in the state of New York. He is also fluent in martial arts and has been training since the age of 12.

- In 2015, Van Halen embarked on a 39-date North American tour with David Lee Roth. This tour followed the release of the band's live album *Tokyo Dome Live Concert* in March of 2015.

- Sammy Hagar wrote and published an autobiography entitled *Red: My Uncensored Life in Rock* in 2011. In April of the same year, the book reached #1 on the *New York Times* bestseller list of hardcover nonfiction.

- In 2019, Eddie Van Halen was hospitalized after having fought throat cancer since 2014, and ex-wife Valerie Bertinelli stated he had also been diagnosed with lung cancer. His health continued to decline, and on October 6, 2020, he died of a stroke at St. John's Health Center in Santa Monica, California. He was 65 years old.

- Prior to Eddie Van Halen's death, Sammy Hagar stated that his hope was for the band to reunite on tour after uncertainty surrounding the band's status was followed by a lack of activity from 2015 to 2019. Hagar stated, "My dream tour is the Sam and Dave tour with Ed, Al, and Mike."

- In a November 2020 interview with Howard Stern, Wolfgang Van Halen announced that Van Halen's days were officially over. "You can't have Van Halen without Eddie Van Halen," he said.

CONCLUSION

After recounting the beginning, middle and end of the fantastic career Van Halen created for themselves, it is undeniable how influential and unique the band really was. Renowned for their dynamic live performances and for bending the "rules of rock," Van Halen's rise to fame was nothing short of legendary.

Lead guitarist Eddie Van Halen redefined the use of the guitar in hard rock in ways that forever altered the industry. While the group has since disbanded, the head-banging, guitar-smashing sound that Van Halen produced will live on through their fans and their influence on the state of music today.

CPSIA information can be obtained
at www.ICGtesting.com
Printed in the USA
LVHW081752130521
687357LV00012B/904

9 781955 149044